THE ALIEN WOOD

T0346173

CAMBRIDGE
UNIVERSITY PRESS

University Printing House, Cambridge CB2 8BS, United Kingdom

Cambridge University Press is part of the University of Cambridge.

It furthers the University's mission by disseminating knowledge in the pursuit of education, learning and research at the highest international levels of excellence.

www.cambridge.org
Information on this title: www.cambridge.org/9781316619896

© Cambridge University Press 1945

First published 1945
First paperback edition 2016

A catalogue record for this publication is available from the British Library

ISBN 978-1-316-61989-6 Paperback

THE
ALIEN WOOD

Twenty Elegies

by

JAMES TURNER

CAMBRIDGE
At the University Press
1945

i

The hands of God reach to the tranquil bays
And shelter;
A movement born of the wind,
Sighing softly in evening under the moonlight,
When earth is ploughed
With the polished steel of the moon,
And water is solid there,
A gleaming silver sword.

The hands of God reach to the tranquil bays
And shelter;
A veil lifted with the fingers
To reveal the golden rods
Of his eternal peace,
When earth is resting,
With the moonlight forking
A centuries pasture with bright teeth,
And trees are statues there
In the wide halls of oblivion.

The hands of God reach to the tranquil bays
And shelter;
A weeping torrent of the willow
Dropping green tendrils to the water

When earth is labouring
With the moonlight raking
A cavern's mouth with dark shadows,
And rocks are ghosts there
With secrets for the grinning skull.

The hands of God reach to the tranquil bays
And shelter;
A grey mould over the sea,
Upon the lonely beach a naked light,
When earth is bringing forth
With the moonlight shivering
An endless crystal of wavelets,
And sea is burdened there
With dark mysteries of eternity,
The hands of God reach to the tranquil bays.

ij

Swans have folded their wings into the lake
          Beneath the languid trees.
The sun is lost. Over this dismal earth
          Falls down no magic pall,
      No silvered carpet nor a curtain gold.

But blistering heat to shrivel up the dead,
And yellow elongated flames to eat the dead,
To shatter death, to ring a mournful bell
          Into the pits of hell.

The human heart is but a solid ash
Blackened of all charity and broken
          Under the fall of masonry,
Under the foolish grin of destruction,
          The hounds of hell.

Here was a palace, here the liquid note
Of blackcap startled in a thicket,
And here a glade where lovers met
To give the living flesh its kiss
Or raise an autumn's lingering lament.

Here now is ash, grey ash of death,
A mask discovered in a prince's hall
And a mantle torn into rags,
            And of doom, the bell.

Singing no more, there is no sound
But of the waters muffled
Where, under languid trees,
Swans have folded their wings into the lake.

iij

Flowers may open on a stricken world,
Bestowing fragrance on the empty lawns,
Giving sweet magic to the lonely house
Wherein a century has held its hour.

And up the stairs a whisper nightly runs,
    'Who comes, who comes?'
A door springs back, the floor is swept,
       'Who comes?'
The moon is fingering the long pale wall,
The rafters ring with long out-moded tones,
A voice is wraithlike underneath the eaves,
      'Who comes?'

The stairs will echo with the ghostly tread
Of children's feet. A cry, a laugh
Will strike a ceiling where no angel sang,
And moon, alone, walks hourly there
To paint the wainscot light and dark again.

The voice cries into a wilderness
Of flowers and scented grass;
Over this stricken earth now moans
    Its spiritless acclaim,
    'Who comes, who comes?'

iv

There is hemlock in the woods
And the soothing syrup of belladonna.
Take these to your lips and so forget
The lonely hours of burning hearts!

What love has brought you here?
Your face a mirage in the snow,
Your fingers icy, but your lips aflame,
What love has brought you here?

O! take this love into your power
Since you are come. Within the glade
Is sign of elfin feet, and a red rose
Has blossomed here in winter,
Where your lips have touched
          That frozen branch.

O! take this love into your power
Since you will go, and going leave
A golden chain to find you in the woods,
To find a home and shelter,
Where the summer dove may rest,
And winter, like this last farewell,
May die away forever into Spring.

V

And stood within an alien wood
A Roman with a silver shield!

The straight road is the road of the dead
Forgotten and unblessed. The berries
In the hedges are of nightshade
        And the killing drops.
Away the year has borne the tender note
Of lark, of sunset liquid tongue,
Away the heritage of fabled voice
Which, with the spring, has toned its echo shrill,
        About the hill
And up the down, where scattered lay
A hundred harebells to a foot of grass.

The straight road is the road of the dead
        And Roman with a silver shield
        Stood silent in an alien wood.

vi

The sea combs out the yellow sand
With the finger of fate. Over
The headland spins the bird
Endlessly weaving life's tapestries.

Into the dark cave-mouth yells the sea
With the moaning of torture,
Under the glowing lights of the ferns
Growing and dying unseen in the labyrinth.
Over the headland spins the bird
Endlessly weaving life's short tapestry.

Into the womb of the green mother
Is sucked back the ever-thirsty water,
Across the thousand golden shells
And the tiny marine creatures.
Down from the headland spins the bird
Performing its circle of life's tapestry.

The sea sucks into the hard rock
And roars upward from the cliff-face,
Pining to escape forward ever
And yet sucked and held back
Upon the milk-white breast,
Up the headland spins the bird
Up into the enamelled dusk.

Farewell into the dying sun,
Shield over shield, white-winged
Pale shadow-flight
Over diaphanous sea,
A two-barbed image
Pointing to the sun in the west.

vij

Deep under the water lie the ancient groves
With temples and statues and the corroded bones
Of men. Under the sea-green water
Tolls the bell and the music
Caresses the high cliff whereon she stands,
Bequeathing her soul into the depths,
Her heart into the forgotten love tales.

The day was fair when she came
Riding horse into those sun-splashed streets,
And golden the roofs and golden
The underfoot. Colours of her women
As the sound of clear cymbals
Across a green meadow where
The pipit nests and the adder
Sways nimbly the standing grass.

And the bell rang in that city
Clear over the headland, over the sea,
Clear into a far country,
From which Fate drew her
Down its spider skein,
Drew her, riding her white horse
Into the city beneath the sea.

Over the dykes paced the wide bosom
Of that swell. City bell returned
The boom of the waves breaking
And booming in that hollow place,
In the dark night when the dove
Sped from the loveless city.

Deep under water lie the ancient groves
Below here where she stands on the cliff,
Bequeathing her soul into the foam-crest
And her heart ablaze with the agèd glory.

viij

The sun stood slanting to the western fields
Where fell the day in that unlucky hour
Of tears, of spells and deep enchantments.

O! you have twisted the golden skein
     And sung the fateful song.
     Youth has taken the sun away
     To die over the crest of the hill.
In the long halls of the crenellated castle
  Stand the idle lackeys of the past,
With the mournful shields and faded tokens
     Of their passing loves,
     Sir Tristram and Sir Launcelot!

Our dreams even are not so invaded
With such luckless loves as these,
Our dreams share death with every moment
Of our waking life. There is a monster
At the gate. I see his lustful eyes
Swinging from dream to life
Bating the breath with the foul odour
     Of the grave.
The trees of heaven were a wonder once
And there were pearls whose touch
Was velvet loveliness, and all the world
Was made to frame this heaven of delight.

But at the gates this monster with his lust
Comes into life, automaton indeed!
A step within, a whisper as of fear
Is heard along the court. Old armour
Rustles in alarm, a helmet falls
Upon the stone-flagged floor;
A mouse retreats into the panelling.

O! the trees of heaven were a wonder once,
And in the candles shone a thousand jewels
Adorning the breasts of saintly women;
The hands of saints were ever red
With blood of their God's wounds.

But who has not heard the stalking foot of death
Along the passage and within the hall?
A skeleton within the breast-plate moans,
He knew thy darkening image on the field
                    Of Agincourt.

Beside the crater grew a tiny flower
And in the chapel ruined by this death,
Where rain had fallen, blossomed in the mould
A yellow flower like to the rose of God.

The sun fell slanting to the western fields,
Sir Tristram and Sir Launcelot turned again
Towards that ancient door of secret locks,
Of tears, of spells and deep enchantments.

A gypsy has passed this way and held
The colours of the setting sun, casting
Its silver sleeves into the shadowed pools,
At noon reflected from kingfisher's throat
On petals of the hollyhocks, but now
                    Dipped to the west
With coming owl and wheeling dusky bat,
Heralding the night in rhythmic circles.

There is a softer light, an hour's glow,
And purple casements in the distant woods;
Something comes stealing at your heels
A perfume made of sun upon the flowers,
Exhaled about the steadfast trunks of trees,
A waiting and a waiting for a gift
That will come tenderly along the shaw
And touch with sleep the heat-engilded flowers.
The world breathes out; there is
A sudden breath as if, in sadness,
A young girl had sighed. Sharp corners
Melt into mist and from the woods
Folds down the cloth of night like gossamer.

The haunted groves and deep enchanted wood
Where moon embezzles of the celandine,
And stars do come to hive within the trees.
And goes from thicket at a midnight hour
The cloak of spangled gold, an ornament
                    Of night.

X

It is not in this hour
When in the hall is sound
Of women's voices
I am created.
There is the smell of night without the windows,
As in the hall swing the skirts
Of the gay dancers over the polished floor,
Breaking the candelabra light
Into sparkling jewels and scattering
Ten thousand pearls at the silver shoes
Of the lovers.
It is not in this hour
I am created
But in the outer darkness
Which is thresholded by light
Of the ball-room windows, pools
Of an oasis of warmth and love.
But in the night
Is hatred and fierce longing
Unabated with cool draughts
Of water, wherein the lips
May drown a false kiss,
Burning as a wound unhealed.

Under night I am created,
Where plays the fountain, touching the marble
With its tiny beads. A bell calls
Along the starlit clouds,
Rings out a bell across the night.

The women dance like phantoms on a screen,
Beneath the trees the ballroom is ablaze.
Louder than the music, clearer than the light,
Within my soul
Rings out a spectral bell across the night.

In the street is the harlot's kiss
And the spike driven through the feet,
The heart crushed by the eternal,
The unending pavement of hard stone.
Dolls are nodding heads in the toyshop.

O! where is the bright spear that shall not be diminished,
   And the golden shield which may reflect the sun,
   The helmet whereon may fall the dying day,
   And the bracelet that may burden out the moon?

In the street is the bright skirt
Of the dancer and the pointed toe
Of a tight-rope walker,
And the hurried pomp
Of vanishing riches.

O! where is the word to lift the chilled heart
   From this hard borne of metal?
   And where the sesame to open the door,
   And to lift this mantled cloak upon the light?

In the street is the song
Of the dead heart broken
On the file, on the rack
Of modern city.

But where the river flows is the swallow's flight
    Above the herbage and the rushes.
    A ship has sailed into the mist
    To the siren-land in a far country.

In the void of night
Is no whimpering of dogs,
Or the wailing of dying women
Adorned in rags whereon is flashing
A gaudy bauble.

In the void of night
Is the howling of a lean wolf
Acquainted with evil
And negation of all good, wherewith
To flaunt a devil.

In the void of night
Is no galloping of hell-horses
Driven through the wild woods
With foam at their jaws,
And the brazen hoof.

In the void of night
Is the whisper of love
Through the crisping leaves
Of the cypress tree.

Here blooms the oleander
Below the shining casements
Of the night. Wax blossoms

Perfume the air with fragrance
Of forgotten dreams.

In the void of night
Is no whimpering of dogs,
But the pregnant womb
Of world-to-come, and of unheard
Reality and Truth.

xiij

Life is compulsion and a holy fire,
A nomad driven on a windy course
   Of beauty;
And of beauty like a livid liquid flame
Lighting the sunset with a crimson pall,
Or darting from the eye of preying lynx
As fire, consuming and consumed.
Of beauty tranquil, beauty childlike,
A feather held upon the palm,
But all compulsion, longing and a wish
To take alone and crush
   And then pass on.

A shrine within a sacred wood
Long overgrown, forgotten, left to fall,
But visited by birds of strange device!

I will compel the very earth to break,
To pour its beauty as a river pours
Over gold-hiding sand,
And strip the edge of the world
Into base fragments to give up
Its mine of secrets.

As the dead rest so shall I,
Encased in secret night
And bedded with the earth.
Spirit shall flame into its contact sure
Of all Life meant. A moment
Will become an age when cruelty
Has perished. And there is sweet rest
Beneath the spacious hands of God
                    In the broad fields.

And the canopy shall be white with fire,
And the banners blaze red with fire
Before the concourse of those coming
Over the radiant heath;
From the mountain, from the sea
Will come the host
To be gathered into the rest of God
Like home-coming of the steel-winged birds
Over the continents.

And it shall be a mortal strife
Made at the grille of death, to take
An iron mask of weird design
To be a god with blood-soaked hands,
And to accept in love this crimson hate,
Which is but facet of a larger jewel
Forming the web of peace.

The magpie has deserted the wood,
The heron flighted to the autumn pool,
     Damp and the winter's rot
Are caretakers of the cold earth,
And a ship with all her sails set
Has filled the harbour's little streets
With the mournful music of the past.

Old and rotting lie the fallen trees
And torn to skeletons the living leaf,
The badger's earth is filled with liquid mud,
     Damp and the winter's rot
Form green mildew like a holy light
And a ship with damask sails set
Splits the gray skirt of water
With the merry laugh of a child's plaything.

The spindle tree burns by the heath
Where, in flocks, the coloured chaffinches
Devour the holly berry, rattling
In brittle cloudlets the burnished leaves
     Of Spanish chestnut.
     Damp and the winter's rot
Are patterns of the woodland carpet,

And a ship with all her sails set
Has sung a mournful melody of love
  Into the sweeping wind.

The fox comes from the old tombs
Over the field-flood to the spinney;
The tower of the church has smoothed
Into mouldering time, escorted
By her halo of ravens. By the gate
An ass has taken the measure
Of her considered world.
  Damp and the winter's rot
Are sped upon their inevitable march,
And a ship with all her sails set
  Whistles her song to dying day
  And the last owl-light.

In the sunlight are the bright wonders of God,
The beamed and moted spearhead,
A javelin from earth to sky;
And the silver mat of the low water
Laid out as a polished reflector
Of the great dome-like doors.

In the sunlight are the bright colours of God,
Where His hand has touched the red flower
Of japonica. There is the jay
Screaming into the wheat, white and red
To the orange of the field and the bullfinch
Splashing its pink into the spring-green hedge.

In the night are the silent spaces of God,
Brought with the spinning bat and paused
With midnight owl and winking stars.
Within the lapislazuli of curtained vault
The road stretches into the silence.

In the night are the silent spaces of God,
The wide bands and the pure chaplets
And a wordless world bemused
In an act of creation.

And night has enclosed the hills,
Night has borne down the valley,
Over the waterfall has night come down
And fallen into the pit.

Sorrow has hidden in the groves,
And with soft weeping has entwined her arms
About the cypress dark and gone
Into the·deepest thickets that she may
Enchain the heart that follows.

Night has borne travail of our sorrow,
Painted the bright pictures with a misty veil,
And made of love a tender memory,
And of herself a permanent reality.

In the night are the bright tears of God,
With the chambers of the sorrowful heart.
The bright tears of God are the gifts of night,
Wherein will He steep His hands
And again be clean.

Over the hills is the white crown
Of the sun, pouring into the valleys
Above the persistent croak of the night-crying frog.

Over the hills is the crown of light
Covering still rivers and the lonely heights,
Above the dew running into her upland basin.

Over the hills is the golden halo
Of dawn. The wide circle is a token
To earth of the broad pastures and green woodlands.

And a dove flew from the wood
Into the valley with the crown
Borne between her gray wings,
And the light in her throat.

xvij

Close my eyes upon the last days of summer
　　And the still trees and the river
　　Where cygnets now float on the water
　　Experimenting with ungainly necks.

　　Here is the farewell flower
　　　　Here in my hand
　　　　As, over the land,
　　Spring thrush sings in the rain
　　Sings and drops down to earth again.

　　Here is the farewell flower
　　　　Laid on the earth
　　　　As, in this new birth,
　　Nightingale sings under the moon
　　Sings and repolishes her silver spoon.

Close my eyes upon the last days of summer
　　When the acorn falls and in the woods
　　Is silence. And in the lane
　　Is the first shiver of autumn.

ere is built the City of God with wondrous music.
　　And quiet within the courtyard is a cloth,
　　A tapestry where dance soft slippered feet
　　Leaving no trace on ornamented floor.
　　The jewelled curtains rise and fall again
　　Into the endless pattern of eternity.

　　There is no more the sealing kiss
　　Or hand touched in the dusk,
　　Or soft breasts folded beneath my hand.
　　　　Now only this,
　　A phoenix from the ash,
　　And God within the burning bush
　　And in the rushing wind.

　　O! take my heart into Thy Heart
　　Dissolve in me all love,
　　That always I may love this subtle scent
　　Grasped here this moment and forever dear.

Dark night falls round me like an evil shroud
　　　　With all its terrors set.
　　　　Wind comes suddenly,
The torching moon speeds through the clouds,
Thus falls the veil; this gift recedes from me
　　　　And thus, alone, I die.

And night enclosed me in its habit dark
                O! heart break now, break now
This is the time for tears if ever shed,
                Bow down my head.
Here on the hill of vision call to the wind
                And none shall answer.
It is not there; it will not come again.

I must go down the hill into the valley,
                Into the burden of Time.
                I must go down the hill.

xix

Through the woods my companion has gone
Beside me, and by the brook
Sat we together, taking measure
Of life, and assessing with love
      The potency of dreams.

But my companion is not of dream-world,
Or of the stuff to weave a children's tale,
Or spin a top, or down the garden path
To bowl a hoop. For children
My companion is the one hiding in hedges
And the secret places of an old attic,
Waiting to spring a trap or to appear
With hideous face from out the cupboard dark.

For they know not the truth of my companion,
How he is always there beside the stream,
Up in the forest where tall trees abound,
Or in the street. Nor have they felt
The warmth of my companion or heard
His voice at night along the lanes
Whispering, 'Come, come with me.'

For my companion is that other self,
Waiting for the journey and for the day
When I, at least, shall not walk the path
To the green river, or see again the Peacock
Sporting on her buddleia tree.

XX

Leaving my love is binding freedom
In chains, and the burden of spring
Into the overheated summer ovens.

The journeys were into freedom
And the faith of love. Of spring
The freedom. Where can I go,
Up here into the hills above the river,
Or here in the woods or again
Along the tessellated street,
And stare and stare without love?

Leaving my love is the closing of hatches,
And to be lost. This was an investment
Of love, this noble building,
This, too, because of our freedom,
This avenue of ilex was an embodiment
Of the straight road of the free.

Who has betrayed? Or must it come
Always to this, a flower grasped
Slowly dying, each minute slowly,
Dying even with soft water?

Where is the meaning of such freedom
And the heart of happiness?

The meaning comes to a betrayal,
Comes to the loss and to iron gyves,
Because her voice sped the hours,
Her laugh was a shield to humour
And her body bought off weariness.

Leaving my love is an open wound
Handwide in my breast and a heart
Of blood sucked dry and of throat
Burning with unslaked thirst.
Leaving my love is a life spent.